# Ministering Spirits

## Engaging the Angelic Realm

**Apostle Stephen A. Garner**

Published by Rivers Publishing Company

Unless otherwise indicated, all scriptural quotations are taken from the *King James Version* of the Holy Bible. All Hebraic and Greek definitions are taken from the *Strong's Exhaustive Concordance*, Baker Book House: Grand Rapids, Michigan

Rivers Publishing Company
Stephen A. Garner Ministries
P.O. Box 1545, Bolingbrook, IL 60440
E-mail: sagarnerministries@gmail.com
**www.sagministries.com**
ISBN - 978-0-9860068-2-1

Printed in the United States of America

# Table of Contents

# INTRODUCTION

There are several weapons the Lord has made available to His Church. He has an armory, according to Jeremiah 50:25, full of weapons which are at the disposal of the saints. The blood of Jesus, praise and worship, intercession, the Word of God, deliverance and healing are all available for the saints to utilize in warfare. Angels are also part of this arsenal in the armory of God. They are released into service through faith-inspired commands, decrees and intercession.

The role of angels in human affairs is undeniable. There are over 300 accounts recorded in scripture from their initial dealings with Adam and Eve in the Garden of Eden to the numerous encounters with prophets of God, including the people of God who made up the Church of the wilderness (Acts 7:38). They have long been at work to assist those who walk in covenant with God. They have been used by God to resist and literally destroy those who dare to stand in opposition of people joined to God in obedience.

The objective of this book is to lay foundation as to why we need angels and their importance in helping us walk out the call of God on our lives. My primary mission is to open the eyes of some and enlighten others to a greater degree of biblical truths concerning these powerful spirit beings. Through the scriptures, we will look at some of their specific mandates as protectors, deliverers and those who benefit from their assistance today.

Angels are both necessary and relevant for the Church of this generation and for the assignments God has given us in the nations. May great grace be released to you and revelation come as you read the pages of this book. My prayer is that the Lord activates a desire in you to utilize the service of these spirit beings sent forth to minister on your behalf as an heir of salvation.

Apostle Stephen A. Garner

# Chapter 1

# ANGELS AS MINISTERING SPIRITS

*Who maketh his angels spirits; his ministers a flaming fire.* Psalm 104:4

*And of the angels he saith, Who maketh his angels spirits, and his ministers a flame of fire.* Hebrews 1:7

*Are they not all ministering spirits, sent forth to minister for them who shall be heirs of salvation?* Hebrews 1:14

Angels are defined as "ministering spirits," according to the referenced verses. The word "minister" means *to aid, serve, supply, care for and attend.* Angels are also "sent forth" to minister. The word "sent" in the Greek literally means *to set apart and send out on a mission.* They have specific responsibilities in the lives and activities of those who are heirs of salvation. They provide and help enforce the Father's will for those who are born again. This being said, every believer is entitled to the benefits of having angels minister on their behalf.

There are several key factors we must look at in order to see the relevance of their ministry today. The first being that they are spirits or supernatural beings, and that their greatest impact is in the spirit world. Scripture states we wrestle not against flesh and blood, yet we are flesh and blood (Ephesians 6:12). So a lot of the warfare and spiritual work we do must be inclusive of angels working on our behalf if we are to have adequate results in the spirit realm.

From the increase of corruption among our political leaders, economic meltdown and terrorism, to the destruction of families and the rise of false religions, the world seems to be overwhelmed. These few areas mentioned have developed problems which exceed man's ability to resolve. Could it be that the answers to these problems are spiritual and require the assistance of angels? Could the lack of the supernatural in the church also have to do with the surge of wickedness in the land; especially that which is being fostered by the ungodly? Even the Lord required angelic assistance. He was pure and had the Spirit of God without measure; yet angels were actively involved in His ministry. The progression of this book will show historically how angels aided and assisted the righteous in times of great distress as some of us are experiencing today.

*And are built upon the foundation of the apostles and prophets, Jesus Christ Himself being the chief corner stone; in whom all the building fitly framed together groweth unto an holy temple in the Lord.*

Ephesians 2:20-21

Churches governed by apostles are able to function and carry out their mandates in specific regions because they have a revelation, just as angels, of being sent. In order for the church to be built properly, fitly framed and grow as a holy temple in the Lord, we need an apostolic and prophetic foundation. If our churches are not built properly God isn't obligated to come and live there, however, He will visit us in His mercy. If we do not build our churches by biblical patterns, we shouldn't expect the same results as those who do because most of the supernatural activity needed to perfect us and strengthen us will not occur, especially the manifestation of angels.

God has set apostles in the church first. This has more to do with function and responsibility rather than popularity. The reality of the spirit world is of no concern to many, and as a result, its threat to our well-being goes unnoticed by many. The Lord Himself functioned as an apostle and dealt a death blow to the kingdom of darkness. And having spoiled principalities and powers, he made a shew of them openly, triumphing over them in it (Colossians 2:15). He has the same requirement for

His church today, we should be duplicating the same work throughout the ages as we consider His apostolic ministry and embrace being sent to serve our cities, regions, nations and generations.

## RELEASE THE DECREES OF HEAVEN

*This matter is by the decree of the watches, and the demand by the word of the holy ones: to the intent that the living may know that the most High ruleth in the kingdom of men, and giveth it to whomsoever he will, and setteth up over it the basest of men.*

Daniel 4:17

This verse shows the powerful role angels have in impacting governments, rulers, kings and kingdoms for the Kingdom of God. The interpretation of King Nebuchadnezzar's dream was declared by the prophet Daniel to be a decree by the watchers and the word of the holy ones (saints). Watchers are powerful angelic beings that function as guardians who deal with the kings of the earth that exalt themselves against the knowledge of God.

The lands of our world are governed by leaders who have brought much confusion and mixture in the earth through their pride and rebellion towards God. The Lord will deal with them and they will know He rules in the kingdom of men. The songs we sing, the praises we release and the proclamations that proceed from our gatherings are all necessary for the release of WATCHERS.

There's a fresh prophetic anointing coming again. The prophets of God will be very instrumental in helping the church overthrow the agenda of darkness in the hearts of leaders who exalt themselves above God and refuse to acknowledge Him. The prophetic anointing serves several purposes in the church, yet one of its greatest is that of helping us to prosper, especially in times of civil and political unrest. Daniel's prophetic influence sent WATCHERS to open the spiritual realm over Babylon so God could deal with the ruling powers of darkness in the life of King Nebuchadnezzar.

## CARRYING OUT EXECUTIVE ORDERS

*And he said, Hear thou therefore the word of the LORD: I saw the LORD sitting on His throne, and all the host of heaven standing by Him on His right hand and on His left. And the LORD said, "Who shall persuade Ahab that he may go up and fall at Ramoth-gilead?" And one said on this manner, and another said on that manner. And there came forth a spirit, and stood before the Lord, and said, I will persuade him. And the LORD said unto him, wherewith? And he said, I will go forth, and I will be a lying spirit in the mouth of all his prophets. And He said Thou shalt persuade him, and prevail also: go forth, and do so. Now therefore, behold, the LORD hath put a lying spirit in the mouth of all these prophets, and the LORD hath spoken evil concerning thee.* I Kings 22:19-23

The prophet Micaiah prophesies the demise of King Ahab; known as one that did more evil in the sight of the Lord than all the kings before him. God was about to bring his reign of terror to an end by the utterance of a prophet who had the aid of ministering spirits sent by God. Micaiah declared the counsel of God's will against Ahab and explained to him how it happened before the throne of God. The hosts of heaven (angels) were gathered before God's throne and an executive order was granted for a spirit being (angel) to go forth and be a lying spirit in the mouth of all Ahab's prophets.

The days have come again where ministering spirits are being sent forth to the heirs of salvation and they are moving at a heightened level to aid the saints in prevailing against the works of the enemy. Ahab was destroyed and the judgments of God prevailed. Today, Ahab is a spirit that drives kings of the earth to negate the influences of the true and living God. The spirit also invokes the assistance of demonic spirits, especially witchcraft, by establishing alliances with diviners and psychics. This spirit of Ahab keeps leaders from embracing the legitimate ways of God and drives them to spiritual whoredoms.

The Church must rise and contend for the fear of the Lord to be restored. We are no match from pulpits or pews in addressing the kingdom of darkness. This battle must be won in the spirit and the aid of ministering spirits is not optional; it is an absolute necessity. Just as Elisha prayed for God to open the eyes of his servant so he could see that there were more for them than against them; I pray for your eyes to be opened to the activity of angels and their mission in the kingdom of God. May faith-inspired utterance come forth through your lips to plant words in the spirit realm and release angels into your cities and regions.

## EXECUTION OF JUDGMENT

*He cried also in mine ears with a loud voice, saying, cause them that have charge over the city to draw near, even every man with a destroying weapon in his hand. And, behold, six men came from the higher gate, which lieth toward the north, and every man a slaughter weapon in his hand...* Ezekiel 9:1-3

Here, Ezekiel is caught up in a vision and God is revealing Heaven's perspective of the activity of His people to him. The idolatrous worship and spiritual perversions have activated the indignation of the Lord. God gives Ezekiel a divine charge in chapter nine to summons those that have authority over the city to judge the idolatrous kingdom that was asserting itself against the purposes of God.

Ezekiel is given the task to call those who have charge over the city to draw near, men with destroying weapons to be exact. The word charge is the Hebrew word 'pquddah,' which in the Hebrew Lexical aid for the Old Testament means *intervention by a superior power (usually God or a king) in order to bring about a great change in the situation of a subordinate.* This vision is depicting a coming of ruling officials (angels) with a mandate to bring about reform into a volatile situation. They have destroying weapons in their hands and the city is being accessed by way of the higher gate. Every city, region, and nation has legal access points (gates) that allow resources to flow in and out.

Deuteronomy 16:18 says, "Judges and officers shalt thou make thee in all thy gates, which the Lord thy God giveth thee..." Gates must be governed by the righteous if ministering spirits sent forth by God are to access our territories. As we pray and intercede over our cities, there are angels who are hearkening to the voice of God's word. If we aren't governing the gates and have not appointed officials at these access points, we won't get the angelic assistance we need.

Six men were given the task to cut off all that had not been marked by the man who had the writers ink horn on his side (See Ezekiel 9:2). They were charged to destroy everything and their eyes were not to spare. I believe this is another principle we must embrace, absolute obedience. This assignment to destroy everything may seem somewhat horrific, but remember we wrestle not against flesh and blood. It is said in warfare that the enemies we leave to remain could very well be the oppressors in generations to come. God is the God of generations and His undying love for us leads Him to take what may appear to be drastic measures, yet absolutely necessary for His purposes to be fulfilled throughout the ages.

Of the judgment released, there was a remnant spared. In a vision, God showed Ezekiel the people sighing and crying out for the abominations that were being done in the land. They are a model for today's prophetic intercessors. They carry the heart of God in the midst of unrighteousness; refusing to submit to the wickedness of their day. If we are to see those who have charge over our cities come and execute judgment, then we must persevere in prayer to cry against the abominations of our day. People who pray with passion and revelation are those who get the job done in the spirit. The Lord himself also holds them in high regard.

*"He cast upon them the fierceness of his anger, wrath, and indignation, and trouble by sending evil (adverse) angels among them".*   Psalm 78:49

The dealings of God upon Egypt (the world) for the injustice of His people were severe. There are judgments reserved for oppressive powers in the earth today which refuse to let God's people go. As it was in those days, so shall it be in our day. The crying and groaning of the saints will ultimately rise to the throne of God and He's going to send His angels to deal with our adversaries as we continue to work in harmony with Him.

## MINISTERS OF REDEMPTION

*Therefore, behold, the days come, saith the Lord, that it shall no more be said, The LORD liveth, that brought up the children of Israel out of the land of Egypt; But, The LORD liveth, that brought up the children of Israel from the land of the north, and from all the lands whither he had driven them: and I will bring them again into their land that I gave unto their fathers. Behold, I will send for many fishers, saith the LORD, and they shall fish them; and after I will send for many hunters, and they shall hunt them from every mountain, and from every hill, and out of the holes of the rocks.* Jeremiah 16:14-16

These verses deal with the physical restoration of literal Israel. As they were delivered from Egypt by the Lord, He also promised to restore them once again from the strongholds of darkness where they were driven to because of their rebellion. This is leading to Babylonian captivity, yet there are some powerful prophetic truths revealed concerning "ministering spirits" as fishers and hunters of men.

In Psalm 144:7, David asked God to send His hand from above and deliver him out of great waters from the hand of strange children. As we begin to invoke their presence in our assignments, these fishers come forth and helped to gather in a harvest of souls in our cities. They are fishing in many waters. There are several references that reveal the different types of waters from which the fishermen shall fish. Psalm 18:16 many waters, Psalm 74:13 waters of strife and Psalm 18:11 dark waters, to name a few. May the Lord send many fishers into your nation and cause them to help gather in the great harvest.

Hunters are also going to hunt them from mountains (stronghold), hills (pride) and holes in rocks (caves of fear). These spirit beings are sent forth to deal with the satanic obstacles that are holding the saints in captivity. Judges 6:12 says, *"And the children of Israel made them dens, caves and strongholds in mountains to hide from Median and Amalek because of fear."* The spirit of fear will cause us to retreat when we need to forge ahead and attack the enemy. The Angel of the Lord declares to Gideon that he's a mighty man of valour. Gideon is ultimately raised up to deal with the enemies of God. Let the mighty hunters of Heaven come forth in the earth to help the church breakout of the barricades of fear so His kingdom can advance through us.

## DISTRIBUTORS OF GOD'S FIRE

*Then flew one of the seraphim's unto me, having a live coal in his hand, which he had taken with tongs from off the altar: And he laid it upon my mouth, and said, Lo, this hath touched thy lips; and thy iniquity is taken away, and thy sin is purged.* Isaiah 6:6-7

The prophet Isaiah had an encounter with the God of Fire during an intense time of worship. A vital part of all believers' development, and especially that of prophets, is a life of worship. One of the ways ministering spirits assist in the developing of prophets is during times of worship. As Isaiah the prophet worshipped, a spirit being, a seraphim took a live coal of fire from the altar before the throne of God. This coal was placed on the lips of the prophet and his iniquity was taken away and his sins purged.

If the prophets of God are going to be able to stand in the counsel of God in this day, they must have encounters with God's fire. The assistance of messengers of fire is even more heightened as we worship. We need them to manifest in times to help deliver God's prophets who are held in bondage and their voices silenced because of iniquity and sin. As the level of our corporate worship increases, surely a cleansing is coming to the prophets by the distribution of God's fire.

Many well-intending people have spoke on God's behalf and have been totally wrong. Thus causing many people, both believers and non-believers alike, to be placed in harm's way and sometimes suffer loss because of an ill-advised spokesman. This has been one of the more disappointing aspects of the church today. People who want to speak for God and are not willing to spend time in His presence lack the ministering of angels and His fire.

Worship is vital because it helps us to appreciate God and honor Him for who He is. As we worship Him, God can strengthen our spirit man in the truth. Lies, error, erroneous ideology, and most of all sin can be subdued and neutralized as we enter His presence. For none of these things can abide in His midst anyway.

Isaiah was able to hear God's voice clearly and embrace his prophetic assignment with a great assurance because of the touch he received from God's fire. Being sent by God, Isaiah's commission brought mighty works in the earth. He was also used to reveal tremendous mysteries concerning our Redeemer; as no other prophet declared. As you press into worshipping the Father, may He begin to reveal His divine purpose to you.

# Chapter 2

# CHRIST AND THE MINISTRY OF ANGELS

*Nathanael answered and saith unto him, Rabbi, thou art the Son of God thou art the King of Israel. Jesus answered and said... Verily, verily, I say unto you, Hereafter ye shall see the heaven open and the angels of God ascending and descending upon the Son of man.*                              John 1:49-51

Nathanael was granted the grace to see heaven open and angels ascending and descending upon the Son of man; based on a revelation of Jesus being the Son of God and King. Revelation is important in receiving from God, as many believers are denied of certain benefits because they lack revelations. Where there is no revelation; people perish. I believe this is true in order to receive of the ministry of angels.

The church is known in the scriptures as the body of Christ. The revelation that must be embraced today is that Jesus lived on the earth in a physical body and He's still alive in a physical body known as the church, which consists of many members from all ethnic groups and nations. This body is ordained to do a greater work in the earth and prevail over the powers of hell because Christ Himself promised that he'd build us. There are several scriptures that support this truth and I've listed a few for your study.

*So we, being many, are one body in Christ...*

Romans 12:5

*Know ye not that your bodies are the members of Christ....*

I Corinthians 6:15

*Now ye are the body of Christ, and member in particular.....*

I Corinthians 12:27

*Who now rejoice in my sufferings for you and fill up that which is behind of the afflictions of Christ in my flesh for his body's sake which is the church....*

Colossians 1:24

*For we are made partakers of Christ, if we hold the beginning of our confidence steadfast unto the end...*

Hebrews 3:14

Some may argue that this was because He is the son of God and it's obvious that He'd have a greater sphere of angelic assistance than that of believers today. However, if we believe God's word based on us being in Christ. we should expect angels to work for us as they did for our Savior when He physically walked the earth. There are a host of scriptures which show angels at work in the Lords life and their relevance in His ministry; from His planting in the womb of Mary to His ascension back into heaven. Our objective is to utilize a few verses to show their importance in His assignment. We are entitled to the same level of angelic assistance today because He now lives in us; we are the body of Christ.

## ANNOUNCE KINGDOM MANDATES

*And the angel said unto her, fear not, Mary: for thou hast found favor with God. And, behold, thou shalt conceive in thy womb, and bring forth a son, and shalt call his name JESUS...*                    Luke 1:30-31

Angels sometimes appear to those who are directly connected to the fulfillment of prophecies and kingdom activity. The Kingdom of God is progressive and in every generation there are people born for set times to help further the agenda of Heaven. God will not be denied of accessing them so He sends angels on assignment.

Mary happens to be one of those people who had a physical encounter with an angel of the Lord. She was chosen to be the one who would give physical birth to our Redeemer. There are many in the earth today who are destined to become impregnated with the purposes of God and ultimately further the Kingdom. Sometimes there are no prophets around to deliver the message and Jesus isn't known to them. So God, knowing how to reach men and women chosen of Him, releases His angels. Consider the visitation of the angel to Joseph and the announcement made concerning the birth of Christ (See Matthew 1:20; 2:19 and Luke 2:8-15), Zacharias concerning the birth of John the Baptist (See Luke 1) and Manoah concerning the birth of Sampson (See Judges 13).

## MINISTERS OF STRENGTH

*Then the devil leaveth him, and, behold, angels came and ministered unto him.....*         Matthew 4:11

Spiritual warfare is inevitable in the life of those who are positioned to advance the Kingdom of God. The Lord was led by the Spirit of God into a battle with the devil. He used the WORD as His choice weapon for war and overcame the temptations of the enemy. The devil appealed to the Lord on three levels. He tried to influence Him in the area of the lust of the eyes (see Matthew 4:2-4), the lust of the flesh (Matthew 4:5-7) and the pride of life (Matthew 4:8-10); also see I John 2:16. After this encounter with the devil, angels came to minister to the Lord.

We may not have had the devil show up to tempt us into sinning against God, but there's an abundance of demons whose sole purpose is to cause the righteous to sin against God by yielding our members to the wicked one. Just as the Lord received ministry from the angels, so should we after intense encounters against the evil one.

*And there appeared an angel unto him from heaven, strengthening him....*                    Luke 22:43

This scripture reveals one of the greatest truths concerning the Lord's preparation for the cross and His commitment for our redemption. He sorted out every challenge in His flesh that was warring against the purposes of God for the generations to come by pressing deep into the place of prayers. Humanity's deliverance was weighing in the balance and the Lord's flesh was looking for a way out of His assignment. God dispatched a powerful angel from Heaven to strengthen His Son.

There are times when breakthrough for the well-being of those to whom we are sent cannot be met by doing what we know. The struggles in our flesh, which are bent on driving us to compromise the call or abandon it all together, require supernatural assistance. This is where the ministry of angels becomes so valuable. The push Christ needed to breakthrough the flesh was ministered to Him by an angel. We can rest assured that just as an angel was sent to minister strength to Christ, that we too can experience their ministry.

## REMOVERS OF BARRIERS

*And behold there was a great earthquake: for the angel of the Lord descended from heaven, and came and rolled back the stone from the door, and sat upon it.*                        Matthew 28:2

The time for our savior's resurrection was at hand. There were satanic barriers present in the form of Roman guards and a stone. The Angel of the Lord descended from Heaven and rolled the stone away. The earth quaked at this coming and his countenance was like lightning. Fear griped the hearts of the Roman guards on watch and they became as dead men.

There are both physical and spiritual barriers that have been positioned by the enemy to hinder us from rising to fulfill the call of God at appointed times. Just as an angel was sent to remove the barriers positioned to stop the Lord's resurrection, so shall they come to assist those found exercising their faith in God for breakthrough.

Today, many churches are forced to operate underground in nations hostile to the message of the gospel. Laws made by oppressive governments force them to gather in secret. The Lord is increasing the activity of angels in the earth and many who are hidden behind satanic structures, which force them underground, are about to experience the Lord's resurrection power. The angels of the Lord are coming to their nations to remove barriers and deal with human opposition. Doors are being opened and the fear of the Lord is being released.

*And there was war in heaven: Michael and his angels fought against the dragon; and the dragon fought and his angels, and prevailed not; neither was their place found any more in heaven.*

Revelation 12:7-8

Satan and his angels once had legal positions in Heaven. But Michael, one of the arch angels, initiated war against Satan and his host of rebels. Satan was then cast out and his influence in Heaven and his position before God was taken away. However, he has come down to earth and established the kingdom of darkness. Along with the establishment of this kingdom, barriers in the spirit realm over the kingdoms of this world have been erected. These barriers are also governed by Satan and his angels.

Barriers are established as mentioned in Ephesians 6 and consist of principalities, powers, rulers of darkness of this world and a spiritual host of wickedness in high places. Their objective is to maintain a level of influence over the church, and at best deny us all together. Their agenda is to influence human governments to rely on their own abilities and deny worship of God or even His existence.

The good news, however, is the Lord has established His throne in Heaven and His Kingdom rules over all. This is a truth the Church must contend for throughout the earth. The Lord is governor among the nations and His Kingdom rules over all. We enforce this through prayer and fasting as we contend with the truth of His word and trust Him to resurrect His body wherever the devil has tried to keep it buried.

## GATHERING OF THE HARVEST

*But when he saw the multitudes, He was moved with compassion on them, because they fainted, and were scattered abroad, as sheep having no shepherd. Then saith he unto his disciples, the harvest truly is plenteous, but the laborers are few; Pray ye therefore the Lord of the harvest, that he will send forth laborers into his harvest.* Matthew 9:36-38

The Lord sees the multitudes (nations) and compassion flows from His heart. Though He's not physically on the planet as the Son of God today, His heart through His church is still full of compassion for the multitudes who don't know Him as their Shepherd. For Jesus has identified the harvest as being His. We, the church, are left with the responsibility of crying out to Him for laborers to be sent forth. These laborers are believers. But on the other hand, they can also be angels as indicated in the verses below concerning the Kingdom.

*Again, the kingdom of heaven is like unto a net, that was cast into the sea and gathered of every kind. Which when it was full, they drew to shore, and sat down, and gathered the good into vessels, but cast the bad away. So shall it be at the end of the world: the angels shall come forth, and sever the wicked from among the just.* Matthew 13:47-49

As the Kingdom of God expands, there is a gathering in every generation. There will be an ultimate separation of that which is of God and that which is of the wicked one. Angels of the Lord have the duty to execute this mandate. We also need them to help carry out the work of separation in the local church today. Certain spirits such as Jezebel, witchcraft, religion, pride and idolatry, to name a few, has been commonly known to creep in and render devastation if it's not separated from among our gatherings.

# Chapter 3

# MINISTERS OF THE COVENANT

*But the mercy of the Lord is from everlasting to everlasting upon them that fear him, and his righteousness unto children's children; To such as keep the covenant, and to those that remember his commandments to do them. The Lord hath prepared his throne in the heavens; and his kingdom ruleth over all. Bless the Lord, ye his angels, that excel in strength, that do his commandments, hearkening unto the voice of his word.* Psalm 103:17-20

God has proven His faithfulness throughout the generations and these verses reveal a key as to how we can experience His faithfulness in our day. He has assigned angels to aid in confirming His covenant. In this section, we will look at some instances where angels moved to confirm healing, deliverance, protection and even answered prayer on behalf of covenant people.

Psalm 103 reveals an angelic pattern for us to follow. Walking in the fear of the Lord and embracing righteous living is the first phase. The next phase is to keep His covenant and observe His commandments. King Solomon, who was one of the wisest kings ever, states in Ecclesiastes 12:13 *"Let us hear the conclusion of the whole matter: Fear God, and keep his commandments: for this is the whole duty of man."* This should be the aim of every believer because the blessings that follow are well worth it. The Lord will prepare His throne in the heavens over your life and the rule of His kingdom will be your portion. The many contentions for our souls that hover over us will become subject to our King. Wherever the throne of God is established, there will be a gathering of the host of heaven, the angels of God (See Matthew 25:31, Revelation 5:11 and 7:11)

The end result for the believer or church that presses into the fear of the Lord and keeps His covenant and commandments is the manifestation of His angels. Once we come into the revelation of their purposes, their intervention in our lives will be unlimited; they impact and touch us in ways unimaginable.

Psalm 103:20 says, they "bless" the Lord, which in the Hebrew literally means *to kneel, i.e. they are reverent and totally committed to the service of God.* They also "excel" in strength which means *they have strength to be matched of no humans.* We are in a war against the powers of darkness and humans alone are no match for demons. However, we have the angels of God who are vibrant in strength and highly intelligent. This verse also states that they do His commandments and hearken to the voice of His word. The one thing that activates them is the spoken word of God. We must speak God's word in faith to see greater angelic exploits in our generation.

## FOLLOWERS OF THE WORD

*And I saw heaven opened and behold a white horse and he that sat upon him was called faithful and true, and in righteousness he doth judge and make war... And he was clothed with a vesture dipped in blood and his name is called THE WORD of GOD. And the armies which were in heaven followed him....*

Revelation 19:11-14

I have taught on the spirit of prophecy from these verses many times (beginning at verse 10) and addressed the fact that the spirit of prophecy caused Jesus or our King to rise in the nations as a man of war. As we prophesy, He will come and deal with our enemies by smiting them with the word of His mouth. Further study on the subject of angels has revealed another truth concerning the ARMIES OF HEAVEN. This army, which consists of angels who confirmed Psalm 103:20, declares they hearken to the Word and now another paradigm is presented where they follow the WORD.

Isaiah 51:16 says, *"And I have put my words in thy mouth, and covered thee in the shadow of mine hand, that I may plant the heavens, and lay the foundation* of the earth, and say unto Zion, Thou art my people". God put His Word in our mouths so that as we speak it, He can plant in the heavens over our territories and release the ARMIES of HEAVEN on our behalf. So as we teach, preach, pray, proclaim, decree and prophesy; we are assured of a divine release on our behalf. What a powerful display of our God who keeps covenant with them who love Him and keep His commandments unto a thousand generations.

## RESPONDING TO THE WORD

*Then said he unto me, Fear not Daniel; for from the first day that thou didst set thine heart to understand and to chasten thyself before thy God, thy words were heard, and I am come for thy words.*    Daniel 10:12

After twenty-one days of fasting and prayer, Daniel has an encounter with a warrior angel named Michael, whom in verse 5 he describes as a man. The angel tells him that he was a beloved man and from the very first day that he set his heart to understand and pray he was heard. He goes on to inform him that his appearance was for the words that were being prayed; remember, the armies of heaven follow the WORD and they hearken to do the WORD.

Daniel is also informed by the angel in verse 13 that there was a delay to his coming because of the prince of Persia. There are times when believers and local churches will encounter strong opposition concerning answers to prayer that will help them forge ahead in their assignments to their generation and those to come. This is another instance where perseverance and a revelation of angels are important. The spiritual opposition that we cannot breakthrough will be broken for us by the angels of the Lord who excel in strength. They are responsible for assisting us and causing us to be victorious. In the case of Daniel, it was the prince of Persia who was interfering with Daniel receiving answers to his prayers. The end result was determined by God because His servant Daniel refused to give into the resistance posed by the powers of darkness unknowingly. As a result, information necessary for the continuance of the plans of God was delivered and the purposes of God prevailed.

## DEFENDERS OF CITIES

*For I will defend this city to save it for mine own sake, and for my servant David's sake. Then the angel of the Lord went forth, and smote in the camp of the Assyrians...* Isaiah 37:35-36

These verses are the climax of a series of exchanges between Heaven and Earth. King Hezekiah heard of the Assyrians plan to invade Israel and topple Jerusalem. He humbled himself with sackcloth and ashes and began to pray. He also sent messengers to Isaiah, the prophet of God, and informed him of what was ensuing. Isaiah released a series of prophetic words because King Hezekiah was pressing in the Spirit to hear from God. This exchange led to God sending His angel to literally wipe out the Earth's most powerful army at that time. The Assyrian army of 185,000 soldiers is destroyed and God's covenant people were sustained and the promise of God to a servant prevailed over the satanic-inspired will of man.

Our cities today are still plagued by darkness and demons that are ravaging entire communities. Murder, gang activity, drugs, political corruption and a host of other wickedness are at work. The principle revealed by King Hezekiah is simple. Boisterous threats by demons should drive us to cry to the Lord and inform Him of what is happening; although He knows everything. We should then also place a demand on the prophetic anointing. The end result was the release of one powerful angel who destroyed the enemy and defended the city because of the WORD and the perseverance of God's servant for help.

*The Lord hear thee in the day of trouble; the name of the God of Jacob defend thee; Send thee help from the sanctuary, and strengthen thee out of Zion.*

Psalm 20:1-2

These verses reveal yet another truth concerning God defending us and sending help in times of trouble. There is also an impartation of strength that will come from Zion as we cry out to our God. Zion is the habitation of God; it is the place where He dwells and also a place where an innumerable company of angels abide revealing a prophetic picture of the New Testament church (See Hebrews 12:22-27).

There are several ways in which angels are sent from the sanctuary to assist us in times of trouble confirming Gods covenant with us.

*They chase and persecute our enemies...*

Psalm 35:5-6

*They are encamped around us to deliver us....*

Psalm 34:7

*They are given charge over us to keep us and bear us up*                            Psalm 91:11-12

*They bring us into prepared places.....*     Exodus 23:20

*They drive out demonic squatters....*      Exodus 23:23

*They give skill to understand.....*      Daniel 9:20-22

*They stir waters of healing in our cities...*   John 5:1-4

*Then the king commanded, and they brought Daniel, and cast him into the den of lions. Now the king spake and said unto Daniel, Thy God whom thou servest continually, he will deliver thee.*

Daniel 6:16

In the midst of certain death, Daniel's life was preserved. The odds against him were reversed and his accusers put to shame because of angelic protection. The decree of king Darius was that no other god could receive prayer; just the idol which he set up. Daniel refused to obey because this decree transgressed the commandment of the only true God. As a result, he was thrown into an actual lion's den. To the astonishment of his accusers, he came forth unharmed. His assurance that God would deliver him from the lion's den was already proven in the third chapter of Daniel concerning the fiery furnace.

The devil is walking about as a roaring lion today and ravaging marriages, children, businesses and even churches. Yet, we have angels who will protect us; if we refuse to compromise the WORD of God. May your confidence prove strong in this day and the angel of the Lord visit you and deliver you from every den of lions.

*At that time Michael, the great prince who protects your people, will arise. There will be a time of distress such as has not happened from the beginning of nations until then. But at that time your people-everyone whose name is found written in the book-will be delivered.*                    Daniel 12:1(NIV)

From a historical perspective, this verse is directly connected to literal Israel and the Jewish people. There are also indicators which reveal that Daniel was referring to a future event that has to do with eschatology; the study of the end-times. However, I'd like to give you just the principles that will help further our case concerning the relevance of angels and their importance today.

This great prince, Michael who protects the people of God, will arise during a time of distress that up to that point the people of God hadn't seen. Remember, Jesus isn't just Savior of some, but the Savior of all the "whosoevers", who will exercise faith in the Word of God and accept Him as Lord. The earth is in a great time of distress and many nations are in turmoil and situations appear to be getting worse. We are not to fret nor become dismayed because God cannot lie and therefore His promise to protect us remains true. Begin to command the release of your angel, for he will hearken to the voice of God's Word as you speak and pray it. Remember our God is supernatural and He gave His best when He sent Christ to die for us, we are assured of victory!

# Chapter 4

# ANGELS AND APOSTOLIC MINISTRY

In writing the book of Revelation the apostle John made reference to the angels assigned to specific churches. In some circles, the term angel has been defined as being the pastor of the churches mentioned by John in the referenced verses below. However, there are over fifty references consistent with angels being spiritual beings who were sent by God to assist the mentioned churches in the book of Revelations. I believe that churches established by God will have the assurance of ministering spirits at their service, especially those governed by apostles.

*Unto the angel of the church of Ephesus.....*

Revelation 2:1

*Unto the angels of the church in Smyrna......*

Revelations 2:8

*Unto the angel of the church of Pergamos.....*

Revelation 2:12

*Unto the angel of the church of Thyatira.....*

Revelation 2:18

In this chapter we will look at how angels directly impacted the apostles of the early Church. There are few detailed accounts that we will refer to from the book of Acts and draw some conclusions from to show how we can benefit from their service today. As you read these points, keep in mind that these believers were full of the Holy Ghost, flowed in the gifts of the Spirit and literally experienced miracles of which we merely preach about. Having said all this, they also enjoyed the ministry of angels and regularly received of their ministry.

The apostolic ministry is one that has many dimensions and spheres of influence; one of them being a ministry of warfare. Many churches have strayed away from warfare and restrained its members from even using language that would suggest warring and fighting through confronting the powers of darkness as a means of advancing God's Kingdom. As stated earlier; apostles are sent with specific assignments to generations, regions and people; with the advancement of God's purposes being the primary objective. The powers of darkness are not simply going to give up control of cities and nations apart from warfare.

*For though we walk in the flesh, we do not war after the flesh; (For the weapons of our warfare are not carnal, but mighty through God to the pulling down of strongholds;) Casting down imaginations and every high thing that exalts itself against the knowledge of God, and bringing every thought to the obedience of Christ;*          II Corinthians 10:3-5

The words strongholds, imaginations and high things are all legal targets of the weapons God has given us for warfare. The key word we want to define is warfare and show why apostolic ministry is geared towards warfare and why apostles should at times be very militant. There are two words in the Greek which define warfare: the first is "strateia" (strat-i-ah) *military service, i.e. the apostolic career as one of hardship and danger, warfare.* The second is "strateoumal" (strat-yoo-om-ahee) *to serve in a military campaign, to execute the apostolate with its' arduous duties and functions. To contend with carnal inclinations, soldier go to war.* From these definitions we can see why apostles and apostolic ministries can appear at times to be very militant and mandate driven. We can also see why apostolic ministry is important and must be embraced in order for the Church to break through and stay current with the movement of the Spirit of God.

The influence of our culture has rendered devastating effects to our credibility as the people of God because we've become so sensitive to the appeal of man and desensitized to the Spirit of God. Warfare is necessary to recapture that which has been lost and apostles are being sent to initiate the restoration of all things. The falling away is because of Satan and we (apostles) are no match alone for him and his demons. Therefore, we must embrace the angelic warriors that God is sending to assist us.

*Then the high priest rose up, and all they that were with him, (which is the sect of the Sadducees,) and were filled with indignation. And laid their hands on the apostles, and put them in the common prison. But the angel of the Lord by night opened the prison door, and brought them forth, and said, Go, stand and speak in the temple to the people all the words of the life.* Acts 5:17-20

Demons will often inspire those joined to religious kingdoms to oppose individuals who are moving in present truth; especially apostles and apostolic ministries. Present truth is simply what the Spirit of God is emphasizing at any given time. In this case, there is a high priest and a company of Sadducees who are filled with anger because of the miracles being wrought by the hands of the apostles. The sick were being healed, demons were being driven out, believers were being added to the church and multitudes were spilling out in the streets. As a result of this, the apostles are apprehended and thrown in prison. God, in His justice, sends an angel to break them free.

There are spiritual prisons that the enemy seeks to place apostles and apostolic ministries in because of the viable threats they pose in the kingdom of darkness; particularly that of religion. Religious spirits hate to see the people of God break free and experience the liberty that Christ paid for us by dying on the cross and shedding His blood for our sins. Anything or anyone who takes away from the notoriety of those under the influence of religion will come under intense scrutiny and persecution. Apostles also have great disdain for religious spirits, as their ministries are geared towards warring against religious kingdoms and therefore angelic aide is vital to them.

*And the angel of the Lord spake unto Philip, saying, Arise, and go toward the south unto the way that goeth down from Jerusalem unto Gaza, which is desert. And he arose and went: and, behold, a man of Ethiopia, a eunuch of great authority under Candace queen of the Ethiopians, who had the charge of all her treasure, and had come to Jerusalem for to worship.* Acts 8:26-27

Philip was one of the original seven deacons and also an evangelist according to Acts 21:8. He benefitted from the ministry of angels by winning a eunuch who happened to be the treasurer to the queen of Ethiopia. There are certain people who will not be able to access and connect because of their importance in the realm of men. However, angels are spirit beings and are not limited as we are. They have a responsibility to help us further the cause of heaven in the affairs of men. Even as Philip was able to utilize their insight and ultimately win the treasurer, so shall we.

*A devout man, and one that feared God with all his house, which gave much alms to the people, and prayed to God always. He saw in a vision evidently about the ninth hour of the day an angel of God coming in to him, and saying unto him, Cornelius. And when he looked on him, he was afraid, and said, What is it, Lord? And he said unto him, Thy prayers and thine alms are come up for a memorial before God.*                                    Acts 10:2-4

Cornelius represents a nation that needs a spiritual upgrade. He was of the Italian band, and a Gentile who possessed God qualities. An angel appears to him in a vision to inform him that his prayers had been answered. He's given instructions on what he needs to do in order to receive an impartation that will upgrade his ministry.

A Jewish apostle named Peter was internally challenged with non-Jews, yet was the one chosen by God to connect with Cornelius. The racial issues that many believers are facing in the nations today definitely require the intervention of God by angelic assistance. The end result was Peter being used of God to do something that directly caused kingdom impact and liberty to come to him at the hands of angelic assistance.

*Peter therefore was kept in prison: but prayer was made without ceasing of the church unto God for him. And when Herod would have brought him forth, the same night Peter was sleeping between two soldiers, bound with two chains: and the keepers before the door kept the prison. And behold, the angel of the Lord came upon him, and a light shined in the prison: and he smote Peter on the side, and raised him up, saying, Arise up quickly. And his chains fell off from his hands.* Acts 12:5-7

It was during a time of great famine and civil unrest that King Herod began to stretch forth his hands to vex certain people of the Church. The suffering of the people was appeased by the murder of God's apostle. During times of social and political decay, the enemy has consistently sought to destroy those who stand for what is righteous. In this case, the apostles were responsible for a mighty shaking in the land and as a result they became targets of the enemy's destructive plan.

James, the brother of John, was killed and now Peter was apprehended and sentenced to death. He was placed in prison awaiting execution, but the saints were stretching out in prayer without ceasing for him. A powerful angel appeared in the night and escorted Peter from prison. There was an iron gate opposing his freedom, which opens to him on its own accord and he is now found on a city street. Peter finally realized that it was an angel and he escaped death at the hands of a wicked king; who was bent on cutting his life short.

Once again, we see the importance of consistent prayer. There is a level of supernatural strength and intervention that is needed, which will not come until we learn to persevere. May you see the increase of angels in your sphere as you continue to press into praying and trusting God for your breakthrough. The latter part of this story shows how God judges the rule of King Herod who sought to be exalted as God. The angel of the Lord strikes him and immediately he's consumed by worms. (See Acts 12:20-23).

May the angels of the Lord be released into your life and assignments as God's plan for your generation continues to be revealed. I decree they strike through kings (demons) for you and help you to further the cause of the Kingdom. I decree that as you pray, more revelation and passion will flood your life and that in all things, you become more effective in the work of the Lord.

In closing, remember that angels and men shall and will bow before our Great King, Jesus. He alone is to be exalted above all.

This teaching is simply a tool to provide additional insight to resources made available to you as a result of the redemptive work of our Savior.

## MORE GREAT RESOURCES FROM
## Stephen A. Garner Ministries

**Books**
- Apostolic Pioneering
- Benefits of Praying in Tongues
- Exposing the Spirit of Anger
- Fundamentals of Deliverance 101, Revised and Expanded
- Pray Without Ceasing, Special Edition
- Restoring Prophetic Watchmen
- Deliver Us From Evil
- Essentials of the Prophetic Revised & Expanded
- The Kingdom of God: A Believer's Guide to Kingdom Living
- Kingdom Prayer
- Prayers, Decrees and Confessions for Wisdom
- Prayers, Decrees and Confessions for Favour & Grace
- Prayers, Decrees and Confessions for Prosperity
- Prayers, Decrees and Confessions for Increase
- Prayers, Decrees and Confessions for Righteousness, Revised & Expanded
- Prayers, Decrees and Confessions for Goodness & Mercy
- Prayers. Decrees and Confessions for Power
- Prayers that Strengthen Marriages and Families

**CD's**
- Prayers For The Nations
- Prayers Against Python & Witchcraft
- Prayers of Healing & Restoration
- Prayers of Renunciation and Deliverance
- Thy Kingdom Come
- Latter Rain
- The Glory
- Overcoming Spirits of Terrorism
- Songs of Intercession
- The Spirit of the Breaker
- The Fear of The Lord

## CONTACT INFORMATION
STEPHEN A. GARNER MINISTRIES
P.O. BOX 1545, BOLINGBROOK, IL 60440
EMAIL: SAGARNERMINISTRIES@GMAIL.COM
WWW.SAGMINISTRIES.COM

Made in the USA
San Bernardino, CA
28 December 2016